Great Disasters

Henry Billings

Melissa Stone

STECK-VAUGHN
COMPANY
ELEMENTARY · SECONDARY · ADULT · LIBRARY

Books in this series:
Great Disasters
Great Escapes
Great Mysteries
Great Rescues

Acknowledgments

Supervising Editor
Kathleen Fitzgibbon
Project Editor
Christine Boyd
Designer
Sharon Golden

Photo / Illustration Credits

Cover Illustration: Floyd Cooper

pp. 2, 3 Brown Brothers; p. 5 Historical Pictures Service, Chicago; p. 8 The Bettman Archive; pp. 11, 12 Brown Brothers; pp. 16, 17 The Bettman Archive; p. 18 Brown Brothers; p. 19 Historical Pictures Service, Chicago; p. 25 Brown Brothers; p. 22 G.K. Gilbert/U.S. Geological Survey; p. 24 Photo Courtesy The Wells Fargo Bank; p. 26 The Bettman Archive; p. 30 UPI/Bettman Newsphotos; pp. 33, 34, 35, 37 Brown Brothers; p. 39 AP/Wide World; p. 41 UPI/Bettman Newsphotos; p. 42 Photoworld/FPG; p. 52 AP/Wide World; pp. 46, 47 Henry Helbrush, p. 47 © S. Lissau/H. Armstrong Roberts; p. 55 © Roger Werth/Woodfin Camp & Associates; pp. 56-57 © Zimberoff/Sygma; p. 60 AP/Wide World; p. 62 © Baldev/Sygma; p. 63 © Zlotnik/Sipa Press; p. 65 © Baldev/Sygma; p. 66, 69 Photos Courtesy NASA; p. 70 AP/Wide World; p. 71 AP/Wide World; p. 74 © Jim Pesco/Yellowstone National Park; pp. 75, 77 © Ted Wood/Picture Group; pp. 80, 81, 83 AP/Wide World.

ISBN 0-8114-4175-X

Contents

Fire! Fire! Fire!

Dennis Rogan went to bed early. He fell asleep quickly in the warm October air. Then suddenly he awoke. He heard shouting.

"Fire!" someone yelled.

Rogan jumped up and ran outside. The O'Learys' barn was on fire. Rogan ran next door to the O'Learys' house. He pounded on the door to warn them. Then he ran for safety. Later, he asked another neighbor how the fire started.

The neighbor said, "Mrs. O'Leary's cow kicked over a **lantern**. It landed in the hay, and now everything is on fire!"

Bad Luck

No one knows if the cow really did knock over a lantern. But one thing is certain. At about 8:45 P.M. on October 8, 1871, fire broke out on the West Side of Chicago. The fire started in the O'Learys' barn. A nearby store owner spotted the fire. He rang a fire alarm. But the message never reached the fire station.

A lookout on the **courthouse** tower also spotted the flames. His alarm did reach the station. But he made a mistake. He thought the fire was coming from a different place. His alarm sent firefighters rushing in the wrong direction.

The bad luck didn't end there. When a fire truck finally arrived at the barn, it broke down. Firefighters could not fight the fire until they repaired the truck.

Lack of rain added to the problem. The summer of 1871 had been very dry. A **drought** had spread over the midwestern part of the U.S. Everything was dry and dusty and ready to burn. To make matters worse, the wind kicked up. A 25 mile-per-hour wind sent sparks flying from house to house.

The fire spread quickly. It ate through the wooden barn and leaped to other buildings. Homes and businesses went up in flames. Almost all of the buildings were made of wood. Sidewalks and fences were wooden, too. So there was nothing to slow the fire down. Thousands of people from the West Side had to leave their homes. They took what they could and ran for their lives.

A City Under Fire

By 9:30 P.M., several city blocks glowed red. The fire grew bigger and bigger with each passing minute. The blaze roared up the West Side. At 11:30 P.M., it leaped across the Chicago River. People on the North Side and South Side had thought they were safe. Suddenly, they too had to run for their lives.

Smoke filled the air. Huge tongues of flames dashed across the sky.

"There were moments I could see buildings melt," one witness said.

Another said, "It was a sea of fire. The air was filled with burning **embers**. The wind blew **fiercely**. Thousands upon thousands of people rushed about, burned out of shelter and without food."

Mrs. Aurelia King told how she ran from the fire. She said, "It was two o'clock in the morning when I **fled**. My little children were clinging to me. The air

was full of burning boards and **shingles** flying in every direction and falling everywhere around us. It seemed as if the whole world was running like ourselves."

Relief at Last

Finally, it began to rain. After 26 long hours, the firefighters were able to put out the fires. By that time, the city lay in **ruins**. Over 2,000 **acres** were destroyed. Property damage was $196 million. Over 100,000 people lost their homes. And about 300 people lost their lives.

Those who lived began to rebuild the city. They brought in famous builders to put up beautiful new buildings. This time they learned from their past experience. The buildings were made with stone and brick. Soon Chicago was once again a busy, lively city.

Do You Remember?

■ In the blank, write the letter of the best ending for each sentence.

_____ 1. The fire leaped across
   a. Lake Michigan.   b. the Chicago River.   c. Hudson Bay.

_____ 2. The summer of 1871 was very
   a. dry.   b. wet.   c. short.

_____ 3. The first fire truck to get to the fire
   a. caught fire.   b. broke down.   c. had no water.

_____ 4. The fire was spread by the
   a. wind.   b. river.   c. horses.

_____ 5. Most sidewalks, fences, and buildings were made of
   a. wood.   b. steel.   c. bricks.

Critical Thinking — Drawing Conclusions

■ Finish each sentence by writing the best answer.

1. Dennis Rogan knocked on the O'Learys' door because _____

   _____

   _____

2. Firefighters rushed off in the wrong direction because_____

   _____

   _____

3. People ran out of their homes because _____

   _____

   _____

Exploring Words

■ Use the words in the box to complete the paragraphs. Reread the paragraphs to be sure they make sense.

lantern	courthouse	lack	drought	embers
fiercely	fled	shingles	ruins	acres

In 1871, a summer **(1)** _____ left Chicago dry and

dusty. The **(2)** _____ of rain caused problems. On

October 8, a fire began to burn **(3)** _____ on the West

Side. No one knew how it started. Some people said a cow kicked

a **(4)** _____ into the hay. A lookout on top of the

(5) _____ reported the fire to firefighters. But firefighters

couldn't stop the blaze.

As the fire spread, people **(6)** _____ from their

homes. They saw **(7)** _____ from the fire flying

through the air. They saw **(8)** _____ torn from rooftops

flying in the wind. By the time the fire died, the city was in

(9) _____ Over two thousand **(10)** _____

had been destroyed.

A City Under Snow

In the darkness of a late March night, a young man hurried along the streets of New York City. A hard, freezing rain poured down on him. Wind whipped at his face and clothes. He shivered and walked faster.

Suddenly a strong **gust** of wind swept by him. It picked up the front steps of a house. The steps went flying down the street.

The man couldn't believe what he had just seen. When he got home, he checked the newspaper. The weather report said that it would be partly cloudy with strong winds, followed by clear skies. The man felt better. Perhaps the gust of wind had been a **freak** thing. But the weather report was wrong. The gust of wind was the start of the worst storm ever to hit New York City. Later this storm, which began on March 11, 1888, would be called the **Blizzard** of '88.

Caught by Surprise

By dawn on March 12, the rain had turned to snow. It fell from the sky as sharp, icy **flakes**. Winds of 80 miles per hour kept the snow **swirling** madly in the air. **Snowdrifts** reached 20 feet or more. Many New Yorkers did not realize how bad the storm was. Looking out their windows, they saw nothing but white, blowing snow. Still, they thought it would end soon. They thought it was just a small snowstorm.

In Harlem, Mrs. Charles Green bundled up her ten-year-old nephew, Sam Strong. She helped him put on his boots, hat, coat, and gloves.

"There, you could go to the North Pole in that outfit," she said cheerfully. "Hurry now, so you won't be late for school."

Sam couldn't see a thing as he walked outside. The wind drove icy snow into his cheeks and down his neck. When he turned onto Lenox Avenue, the wind grabbed him and threw him into the air. He landed in a deep snowdrift. The snow was way over his head. Sam tried to move his hands and feet. He tried to dig himself out of the drift. But he couldn't. Five minutes passed. Then ten. Then fifteen. Panic began to sweep over him. He feared he might die buried in the snow.

One of the Lucky Ones

At last a police officer passed the snowdrift. He heard young Sam's cries. The officer clawed away at the snowdrift. Finally, he reached Sam and pulled him out.

"You shouldn't be out in this, Sonny," he said. "You go straight home."

It took Sam hours to get back home. His ears were stinging. His face hurt. He barely had enough energy to crawl through the drift to his front porch. But he was one of the lucky ones. The blizzard caused nearly 100 people to die that day in New York City alone.

A City Buried in Snow

All over the city, things came to a sudden stop. Milk couldn't be delivered, so babies went hungry. Because coal deliveries stopped, families could not heat their homes. Street cars and cabs stopped running. Thousands of workers had no way to get home.

As the day went on, the city took on an **eerie** look. The wind **flung** boxes, signs, and benches down the street. Thousands of sparrows dropped from the sky. They had frozen. Horses, too, lay dead in the streets. Many were still tied to the wagons they had been pulling.

And still the blizzard did not stop. People staggered through the streets, looking for open grocery stores. The icy snow cut at their faces until they bled. At stores they bought gloves and shovels. They begged for food and coal.

Later, these people searched for words to describe the snow and wind.

"It felt like lashes of a whip," said one person.

"The air was full of fine needles of snow," one man remembered. "The **sleet** striking my face made me feel as if it was raining carpet tacks. Little **icicles** formed on my eyelashes and got into my eyes. They felt like hot cinders."

The End of the Blizzard

By the third day, the blizzard started dying down. The wind dropped, and the snow stopped falling. That afternoon the sun poked through the clouds. Slowly, New York City came to life again.

The blizzard was over. But the memory of it stayed. The storm had destroyed homes all along the East Coast. It did $20 million worth of damage in New York City alone. It also took the lives of almost 300 people.

Those who lived never forgot it. Certainly Sam Strong never did. The little boy who almost died in the snowdrift went on to become head of the Society of Blizzard Men and Blizzard Ladies. Every year he met with other people who had lived through the storm. As long as he lived, he never forgot the force of the wind that March day. He never forgot the terror of being trapped in a huge mountain of snow. And he never forgot the kind police officer who saved his life.

Do You Remember?

■ Read each sentence below. Write **T** if the sentence is true. Write **F** if the sentence is false.

_____ 1. The blizzard started as a hard, freezing rain.

_____ 2. Snowdrifts reached 20 feet.

_____ 3. Sam Strong almost died in a river.

_____ 4. Milk was delivered as usual.

_____ 5. Thousands of sparrows froze.

_____ 6. The blizzard lasted less than 24 hours.

_____ 7. The blizzard did very little property damage.

_____ 8. People who lived through the blizzard never forgot it.

Express Yourself

■ Pretend you are Sam Strong. You have just made it home after being saved by the police officer. Write an entry in your journal telling about this day.

_____

_____

_____

_____

_____

_____

Exploring Words

■ Read each sentence. Fill in the circle next to the best meaning for the word in dark print. If you need help, use the Glossary.

1. A **gust** of wind blew the steps off a house.
   ○ a. steady force   ○ b. small amount   ○ c. sudden blast

2. The blizzard was **freak** weather.
   ○ a. good   ○ b. unusual   ○ c. exciting

3. People had no warning that a **blizzard** was coming.
   ○ a. heavy snowstorm with high winds
   ○ b. thunderstorm
   ○ c. dust storm

4. Icy **flakes** cut people's faces.
   ○ a. small bits of snow   ○ b. winds   ○ c. drops

5. The high winds kept the snow **swirling** in the air.
   ○ a. hanging   ○ b. moving   ○ c. freezing

6. Sam had trouble getting through the deep **snowdrifts**.
   ○ a. piles of snow   ○ b. snowstorms   ○ c. puddles

7. The dark streets looked **eerie**.
   ○ a. strange   ○ b. quiet   ○ c. dangerous

8. The wind **flung** signs to the ground.
   ○ a. flew   ○ b. stretched   ○ c. threw

9. During the first night, the rain turned to **sleet**.
   ○ a. icy rain   ○ b. gentle mist   ○ c. soft snow

10. **Icicles** stuck to one man's eyelashes.
    ○ a. drops of rain   ○ b. spikes of ice   ○ c. frost

Washed Away!

The rain poured down all night. Rivers flowed over their banks. Main Street was already underwater. By noon on May 31, 1889, some of the people of Johnstown, Pennsylvania, had seen enough. They left for higher ground. Most, however, stayed put. They had been through flood scares before.

A Dam Made of Dirt

Fourteen miles up the valley from Johnstown, stood the South Fork **Dam**. It was built with dirt in the 1840's, and it held back a huge lake. A break in the dam would flood the whole valley. This worried some people. After all, how long could a dam made of dirt last?

Daniel Morrell was one of the most important people in Johnstown. Morrell sent an engineer to look at the dam. The engineer reported a big leak and said the dam needed to be repaired.

Morrell wrote letters to the dam's owners, begging them to fix the dam. But the owners lived far away, in Pittsburgh. They were not worried about the dam. One owner wrote to Morrell, "You and your people are in no danger from our **enterprise**." Morrell wrote back that the dam was dangerous to the lives and property of all those living in the valley.

Morrell died in 1885. Four years later, his worst **nightmare** came true.

Disaster Strikes

The heavy rains had filled the lake. At 3:10 P.M. on May 31, it happened. The dam gave way.

Twenty million **tons** of water exploded down the valley, wiping out everything in its path. Along the way, the flood picked up hundreds of trees, houses, and boulders. The flood crashed through the small town of Woodvale in five minutes, killing 314 people. Only one building was left standing.

Johnstown was next in the flood's path. It took about ten minutes for the **raging** waters to destroy the town. People did what they could to save themselves. Some ran for higher ground. Others **clung** to floating rooftops. Still others ran for the strongest-looking building they could find.

Help Arrives

Six-year-old Gertrude Quinn was on the third floor of her house when the flood struck. The house trembled as the water pounded against the walls.

Gertrude managed to climb up on the roof. She jumped onto a mattress that was floating by just as her house was swept away.

Luckily, **debris** beneath the mattress kept it floating. Night was approaching. Gertrude was **terrified**. A dead horse slammed into her raft.

The six-year-old floated by a large building with people crowded on the roof. She screamed for help. A mill worker named Maxwell McAchren heard her. He dived into the water. His head bobbed up and down in the strong **current**. Several times he went under. But at last he climbed onto the mattress.

Together, the two floated along. Suddenly, they saw two men on a hillside about ten feet away. The men were trying to help people. One of the men shouted, "Throw that baby over here to us."

McAchren picked up Gertrude. Using all his strength, he threw the little girl to the shore. One of the men caught Gertrude. McAchren had saved the little girl's life. Later, he also managed to save himself.

Starting Over

By the morning of June 1, the flood was over. It left behind a sea of debris and **death**. About 2,200 people had died. Thousands of people had no homes. There was little food or medicine. There was no gas or electricity.

Soon help began pouring in from around the country. People sent food, clothing, candles, blankets, and lumber. The Army and the Red Cross came to help. Slowly, the people of Johnstown brought their town back to life. But they never rebuilt the South Fork Dam.

Do You Remember?

■ In the blank, write the letter of the best ending for each sentence.

_____ 1. The South Fork Dam was built with
   a. bricks.　　b. steel.　　c. dirt.

_____ 2. The dam owners lived in
   a. Pittsburgh.　　b. Johnstown.　　c. Woodvale.

_____ 3. Gertrude Quinn jumped onto a
   a. horse.　　b. mattress.　　c. railroad car.

_____ 4. Maxwell McAchren threw Gertrude to two men
   a. on a roof.　　b. in a tree.　　c. on the shore.

_____ 5. The flood killed about
   a. 200 people.　　b. 2,200 people.　　c. 20,000 people.

Critical Thinking—Fact or Opinion?

■ A **fact** can be proven. An **opinion** is a belief. Opinions cannot be proven.

Write **F** before each statement that is a fact. Write **O** before each statement that is an opinion.

_____ 1. People who lived in Johnstown were foolish.

_____ 2. Daniel Morrell wrote letters to the owners of the dam.

_____ 3. The South Fork Dam was built in the 1840's.

_____ 4. Daniel Morrell should have fixed the dam himself.

_____ 5. The flood hit Woodvale first.

_____ 6. Gertrude was the luckiest girl in the world.

_____ 7. Maxwell McAchren liked to swim.

_____ 8. Many people crowded onto rooftops.

Exploring Words

■ Use the clues to complete the puzzle. Choose from the words in the box.

dam
enterprise
nightmare
ton
raging
clung
debris
terrified
current
death

Across

4. movement of water
5. rushing wildly
6. end of life
9. bad dream
10. scattered trash

Down

1. held on
2. very frightened
3. business
7. 2,000 pounds
8. wall to hold back water

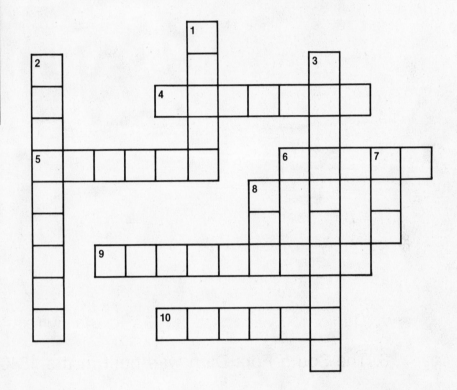

A City in Ruins

James Hopper didn't sleep well. He was having a nightmare. He heard the sound of horses running. The noise kept getting louder and louder. Then a loud roar shook Hopper out of his bed. A real nightmare had just begun.

The surprised reporter rushed to his hotel window. The building was moving from side-to-side. Hopper heard the roar of bricks coming down. The rear of the three-story building was falling. It crushed the wooden houses below. This is death, Hopper thought. He waited to see what would happen next.

The Big Earthquake

It was early in the morning of April 18, 1906. The birds were singing. A thin moon hung in the sky. The morning weather report said, "Fair and warmer." It was 5:12 A.M.

Then, without warning, it happened. The earth began to shake **violently**. Streets rolled like waves in the ocean. Buildings swung violently from side-to-side and then crashed to the ground.

The **earthquake** lasted 40 seconds. Ten seconds of silence followed. Then a second earthquake, equal to the first, shook the city. Trains were tossed on their sides. People died instantly as they were crushed under **rubble**. Some of those who lived found that their fourth-floor windows were now level with the ground.

The streets quickly filled with people. Most were still in their pajamas. Strange sights were seen everywhere. One man ran along the street with his coat and hat. But he had forgotten his pants. A woman wandered through the streets. She carried a birdcage with four kittens in it. A black bull, freed by the earthquake, ran down the street.

Some people stood in **shocked** silence. Others wanted to talk. Maybe if they talked, they could make some sense out of what had happened.

"Quite a rocker, wasn't it?"

"She'll have to shake harder than that to bring this town down."

"Not as bad as the quake in '68."

That was brave talk. But in truth, this was the worst earthquake ever to hit the United States. And the earthquake caused other problems. It broke gas lines and brought down telephone wires. Worst of all, it broke the main water pipes.

Raging Fires

In just a few minutes, dozens of fires started. Because of broken pipes, there was no water to fight the fires. Flames shot up from one end of the city to the other.

Fire horses and engines clattered toward the fires. Firefighters ran from one **hydrant** to another. Sometimes they would find a hydrant that worked. At other times they would use a well. But many times there was no water to be found.

The flames jumped from housetop to housetop. Smoke climbed high above the city. A large, black cloud of smoke could be seen one hundred miles away.

People grabbed blankets or clothes from their homes. They sat outside their homes waiting. When the fires came too close, they left. Sadly, they dragged whatever they could behind them.

The **refugees** sat on hilltops watching the fires come toward them. The fires formed a wall three miles long. When the refugees could feel the heat on their faces, they moved on again. There were 250,000 people now without homes.

The fires took everything in their paths. Chinatown went. So did famous buildings. Flames burned The Emporium, the largest store in the West. Fire shot

up the eighteen-story Call Building. It exploded like a firecracker. San Francisco was burning to death.

Fighting Back

The mayor of San Francisco was Eugene Schmitz. Many people saw him as a weak leader. But he came out of this **crisis** a hero. He laid down the law. In a strong voice, he gave his orders.

"Is **looting** a problem? Protect people's property. Order the police and the Army to kill all persons found looting."

"Are people drinking and causing trouble? Then close the liquor stores. **Forbid** the sale of alcohol."

"What about the fires, sir?" someone asked. "There's no water to fight the fires."

"We'll use **dynamite**," Schmitz ordered. "Get dynamiters from the Army. They can blow up buildings in the path of the flames. That will help stop the fires. When the fires reach the ashes, they'll burn themselves out."

But the dynamite didn't help much. The fires burned on for three days. They turned 510 city blocks into ashes. There was $500 million in property damage and nearly 700 people dead. Four-fifths of San Francisco was destroyed.

Finally, it was over. Slowly people began to walk back into the city. They picked their way through the ruins. The place was a mess. But the people were not about to give up on their town. They began picking up the rubble. The bricks were still hot and burned their hands. But they could not wait. They took off their coats and rolled up their sleeves.

"Let's go," they said. "Let's get started."

San Francisco would live again.

Do You Remember?

■ Read each sentence below. Write **T** if the sentence is true. Write **F** if the sentence is false.

_____ 1. The earthquake happened at noon.

_____ 2. The earthquake lasted for hours.

_____ 3. Many fires broke out after the earthquake.

_____ 4. There were 250,000 people who lost their homes.

_____ 5. Chinatown was not damaged.

_____ 6. Mayor Schmitz ordered the Army to use dynamite.

_____ 7. Most of San Francisco was destroyed.

_____ 8. San Francisco would live again.

Express Yourself

■ Pretend that you are James Hopper. Write an article for a magazine. Describe what it felt like to live through the earthquake.

_____

_____

_____

_____

_____

_____

Exploring Words

■ Use the words in the box to complete the paragraphs. Reread the paragraphs to be sure they make sense.

crisis	rubble	shocked	hydrant	violently
forbid	dynamite	refugees	earthquake	looting

The **(1)** _____ hit early in the morning. The ground

shook **(2)** _____. People were **(3)** _____ to

see buildings fall. Then the city faced a new **(4)** _____

Fire raced through the city. Firefighters hooked up hoses to

any **(5)** _____ that would work. People became

(6) _____ as they left their homes, running from the

fires. Some people began **(7)** _____ stores.

Mayor Schmitz took action. **(8)** "_____ the sale

of alcohol," he ordered. He also asked the Army to bring in

(9) _____. At last the fires stopped. People picked

through the **(10)** _____. They began to build the great

city again.

Nightmare at Sea

Captain Edward Smith stared out into the cold, still night. He had been given the honor of taking the Titanic on her very first trip. After this trip, Smith planned to **retire.**

Smith told the **lookout,** Frederick Fleet, about the reports of ice he had received. Then he went inside the ship to dinner.

Fleet searched the darkness. His job was to watch for **icebergs.** Fleet watched carefully, but he wasn't really worried. The Titanic was the biggest, strongest, safest ship ever built.

All at once, Fleet saw a black shadow right in front of the ship. It was an iceberg! Quickly he rang the warning bell.

Bad News

For the next 37 seconds, Fleet stood frozen as a mountain of ice came closer. The crew tried to steer the ship out of the way. But it was no use. At 11:40 P.M. on April 14, 1912, the iceberg tore a hole in the side of the Titanic. Slowly, the huge **unsinkable** ship started to sink.

Word of the accident spread quickly through the ship. The passengers were confused but not upset. They thought this was a new adventure. A few crew members knew better. The ship's carpenter had been near the bottom of the ship when the 80-foot iceberg hit. He rushed upstairs.

"She's taking water fast!" he called to Captain Edward Smith.

A mail clerk also came running. He announced that water was filling the mail room.

Captain Smith went to check the sixteen **watertight compartments** at the bottom of the ship. These rooms were supposed to keep the ship from sinking. The Titanic should float even if three or four of them filled with water.

Captain Smith found that five of the rooms had been torn open by the iceberg. They were now hopelessly flooded. Water was filling the other rooms as well. There was no doubt about it. The Titanic was going down.

Women and Children First

On the deck, crew members hurried to get out the **lifeboats**. No one knew exactly what to do. They had never had a practice drill. It had not seemed necessary. Finally, they got the first boat ready. Captain Smith called out the order.

"Women and children first!"

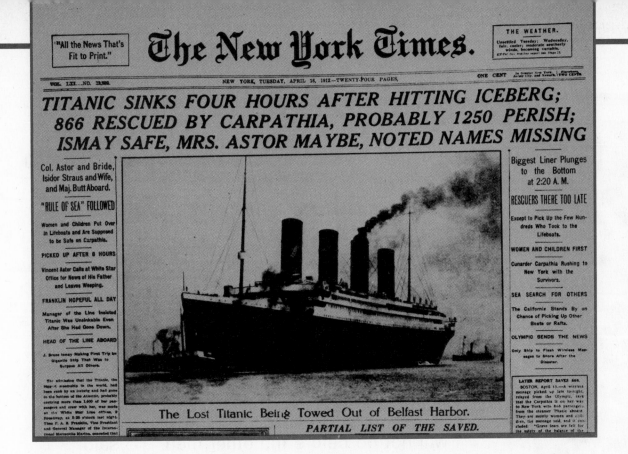

"All the News That's Fit to Print."

The New York Times.

THE WEATHER.
Unsettled Tuesday; Wednesday, fair, cooler; moderate southerly winds, becoming variable.

VOL. LXI—NO. 19,530. NEW YORK, TUESDAY, APRIL 16, 1912—TWENTY-FOUR PAGES. ONE CENT In Greater New York, Jersey City and Newark. TWO CENTS

TITANIC SINKS FOUR HOURS AFTER HITTING ICEBERG; 866 RESCUED BY CARPATHIA, PROBABLY 1250 PERISH; ISMAY SAFE, MRS. ASTOR MAYBE, NOTED NAMES MISSING

Col. Astor and Bride, Isidor Straus and Wife, and Maj. Butt Aboard.

"RULE OF SEA" FOLLOWED

Women and Children Put Over in Lifeboats and Are Supposed to be Safe on Carpathia.

PICKED UP AFTER 8 HOURS

Vincent Astor Calls at White Star Office for News of His Father and Leaves Weeping.

FRANKLIN HOPEFUL ALL DAY

Manager of the Line Insisted Titanic Was Unsinkable Even After She Had Gone Down.

HEAD OF THE LINE ABOARD

J. Bruce Ismay Making First Trip on Gigantic Ship That Was to Surpass All Others.

The admission that the Titanic, the biggest steamship in the world, had been sunk by an iceberg and had gone to the bottom of the Atlantic, probably carrying more than 1,600 of her passengers and crew with her, was made at the White Star Lines offices, 9 Broadway, at 8:20 o'clock last night. Then P. A. S. Franklin, Vice President and General Manager of the International Mercantile Marine, conceded that

The Lost Titanic Being Towed Out of Belfast Harbor.

PARTIAL LIST OF THE SAVED.

Biggest Liner Plunges to the Bottom at 2:20 A. M.

RESCUERS THERE TOO LATE

Except to Pick Up the Few Hundreds Who Took to the Lifeboats.

WOMEN AND CHILDREN FIRST

Cunarder Carpathia Rushing to New York with the Survivors.

SEA SEARCH FOR OTHERS

The Californian Stands By on Chance of Picking Up Other Boats or Rafts.

OLYMPIC SENDS THE NEWS

Only Ship to Flash Wireless Messages to Shore After the Disaster.

LATER REPORT SAVES 866.
BOSTON, April 15.—A wireless message picked up late to-night, relayed from the Olympic, says that the Carpathia is on her way to New York with 866 passengers from the steamer Titanic aboard. They are mostly women and children, the message said, and it concluded: "Grave fears are felt for the safety of the balance of the

But most women and children refused to go. They felt safer staying on the big warm ship. They didn't want to go out into the cold darkness. They didn't trust the small boats. Many still did not believe the ship was in danger.

"Hurry! Hurry! There's no time to lose!" a crew member shouted.

But few people listened to him. An hour later, only 20 people were in the first lifeboat. There was room for 45 more people, but the crew could wait no longer. At 12:45 A.M., they lowered the half-empty lifeboat into the water.

Cowards and Heroes

Finally, people understood that the Titanic was sinking. Suddenly, everyone wanted to get into a lifeboat. But there were not enough to go around. There were 2,207 people on the Titanic. But there were only enough lifeboats for 1,178 people.

The **shortage** of lifeboats brought out the worst in some people. One man snuck into a lifeboat dressed as a woman. Others pushed ahead of mothers and small children. Some men had to be dragged kicking and screaming out of the boats.

But while some people became cowards, others became heroes.

Dr. W.T. Minahan helped his wife into a boat, then stepped back to make room for someone else. "Be brave," he called to his wife. "No matter what happens, be brave."

Someone else tried to help an older man named Isidor Straus into a lifeboat. But Straus shook his head.

"I will not go before the other men," he said.

Mrs. Straus, like many other women, refused to leave her husband. "We have been living together for many years," she said. "Where you go, I go." Then the two of them sat down in deck chairs to wait for the end together.

A Sad End

On the deck, the ship's band played. None of these men had tried to leave. They felt it was their duty to stay with the ship. They did their best to comfort the passengers. They played loud, cheerful music.

By 2:00 A.M., all of the lifeboats were in the water. There wasn't much hope left for those still on the ship. Some jumped into the water. They tried to swim out to the lifeboats. A few made it. But most quickly died in the freezing water.

One swimmer looked back and saw Captain Smith standing on the ship. The water was up to his waist.

Captain Edward Smith

The **bow** of the ship was underwater. The **stern** was up in the air.

At 2:18 A.M. with the band still playing, the stern of the Titanic slid into the water. The great ship sank to the bottom of the ocean, taking more than 1,500 people with it.

A Call for Help

The Titanic's radio operator had called for help on the ship's radio. Several ships heard the cries for help and sailed to her as fast as they could.

The Carpathia was the first ship to arrive. Its crew began picking up the people in the lifeboats at 4:10 A.M. Of the 2,207 people who had sailed on the Titanic, only 711 were still alive.

The Titanic became a legend. For 73 years, people searched for the remains of the great ship. Finally, on September 1, 1985, a team of French and American explorers found her. The rusty wreck lay two miles under the Atlantic Ocean. She was no longer the beautiful and graceful ship she had once been.

Do You Remember?

■ Read each sentence below. Write **T** if the sentence is true. Write **F** if the sentence is false.

_____ 1. The Titanic hit an iceberg.

_____ 2. Captain Smith ordered his crew to get into lifeboats.

_____ 3. There were not enough lifeboats for everyone.

_____ 4. Frederick Fleet was the ship's carpenter.

_____ 5. Every lifeboat was packed full of passengers.

_____ 6. Mr. Isidor Straus snuck onto a lifeboat dressed as a woman.

_____ 7. The band played songs as the Titanic sank.

_____ 8. None of the passengers were saved.

Critical Thinking — Main Ideas

■ Underline the two most important ideas from the story.

1. The Titanic sank after it hit an iceberg.

2. Captain Smith was planning to retire.

3. The mail room was filled with water.

4. The Carpathia was the first ship to arrive.

5. Many people died because there were not enough lifeboats.

Exploring Words

■ Write the correct word in each sentence.

retire	lookout	icebergs	unsinkable	watertight
compartments	lifeboats	shortage	bow	stern

1. Big blocks of ice floating in the ocean are called _____.

2. When there isn't enough of something, there is a _____.

3. If something is _____, water cannot get in or out of it.

4. A _____ watches for danger.

5. The front part of a ship is called the _____.

6. _____ are small boats which people use if they

   have to leave the main ship.

7. If something cannot sink, it is called _____.

8. _____ are small, separate rooms.

9. The back part of a ship is called the _____.

10. Captain Edwards was almost ready to _____.

Flames in the Sky!

"**H**ere it comes, ladies and gentlemen. And what a sight it is, a thrilling one, a **marvelous** sight."

So began Herbert Morrison, an announcer for radio station WLS. He was calmly describing the **airship** Hindenburg. It was just about to land at Lakehurst, New Jersey, on May 6, 1937. Morrison was one of the reporters there to cover the story.

Suddenly, Morrison's voice filled with fright. "It's burst into flames! It is burning, bursting into flames and is falling! Oh! It's a terrible sight! The flames are 500 feet into the sky!"

An Ordinary Trip

On May 3, 1937, the Hindenburg left Frankfurt, Germany. It carried 38 passengers and a crew of 59. The giant airship had already made ten trips across the Atlantic Ocean to the United States. This looked like another ordinary trip.

At first, the flight went smoothly. But as the Hindenburg neared Lakehurst, the weather turned bad. Black clouds gathered. Thunder rumbled. The wind began picking up. Captain Max Pruss didn't want to **risk** a landing. He would stay where he was and wait for better weather.

At last a message came from Lakehurst that all was clear and waiting. The Hindenburg headed for Lakehurst. It seemed that the three-day trip was safely over. Passengers gathered their belongings. They checked their passports. Some looked out the windows. Family and friends waved from the ground. Everyone was smiling.

At 7:21 P.M., landing ropes were lowered from the airship. Captain Pruss sent a message. The message read: "The Hindenburg has just made a safe landing." Nothing could have been further from the truth.

The Safest Aircraft

Until 7:25 P.M., May 6, 1937, no one doubted the Hindenburg's safety. The builders of the airship were proud of their perfect safety record. Not one of their airships had crashed. The Hindenburg was the safest yet. The huge **blimp** measured 146 feet high and 803 feet long. People looked up in wonder whenever it passed overhead. They believed that one day thousands of people would travel by airship.

The Hindenburg had only one weakness. It was filled with **hydrogen**, a gas that exploded easily. One spark could cause the whole airship to explode.

So the crew made sure there were no sparks. No passenger could carry matches or lighters. There was a special room for smoking. It was sealed with two locked doors. Passengers wore sneakers or felt boots to **prevent** sparks. Crew members who worked near the gas cells wore no buttons or metal because of the danger of sparks. They left nothing to chance.

The Accident

The Hindenburg was ready to land. It hung quietly in the air about 75 feet above the ground. At 7:25 P.M., W.W. Groves, an engineer on the ground, noticed something strange. There was a small spark dancing near the stern. "It looked like **static electricity**," he later said.

Suddenly, a huge flame burst from the top of the airship. One of the gas cells in the tail exploded. Within seconds, another cell did the same. People on the ground ran for their lives.

"The whole tail section burst into flames," Groves remembered. "I began to run. It was exploding above my head. Burning **fabric** began to fall."

Meanwhile, in the control car, Captain Pruss felt the airship jerk. He wasn't sure what it was. Perhaps a landing rope snapped, he thought. Then he heard

a loud bang and people screaming on the field below.

"What is it?" he asked, looking out the window.

"The ship's burning!" cried the radio officer.

On the ground, Herbert Morrison, the radio announcer, couldn't believe his eyes. "This is the worst thing I've ever witnessed," he said.

Run for Your Life

It looked like no one could live through the fire. But somehow 62 people did. It took 34 seconds for the burning wreck to crash to the ground. This gave some people time to jump to safety. Passenger Philip Mangone tried to open a window. It was stuck. So he took a chair and broke the glass. Then he jumped 35 feet to the ground. The fire burned his face and hands. But he had no other **injuries**.

Werner Franz, a fourteen-year-old cabin boy, made the most unlikely escape. The fire was all around him. Franz thought he was finished. Just then, the heat caused a water tank to burst over his head, and it soaked him. The water saved him. He managed to escape without being badly burned.

But others did not make it. In all, 36 people died. That included 22 crew members, 13 passengers, and one member of the ground crew.

What caused the crash? It may have been static electricity. It may have been lightning. Some people even think that the fire was set on purpose. No one knows for sure.

Today, airships use **helium**. Helium does not explode as easily as hydrogen. One thing, however, is certain. Because of the crash of the Hindenburg, airships were never again used for passenger travel.

Do You Remember?

■ In the blank, write the letter of the best ending for each sentence.

_____ 1. The Hindenburg was filled with
  a. hydrogen.   b. oil.   c. water.

_____ 2. Passengers were not allowed to carry
  a. sneakers.   b. combs.   c. matches.

_____ 3. Captain Pruss did not want the Hindenburg to land in
  a. New Jersey.   b. May.   c. bad weather.

_____ 4. The radio announcer was
  a. shocked.   b. calm.   c. hurt.

_____ 5. People escaped by
  a. jumping to safety.   b. screaming.   c. standing still.

Express Yourself

■ Pretend that you are Werner Franz. Write a journal entry telling what happened to you the day the Hindenburg crashed.

_____

_____

_____

_____

_____

_____

_____

_____

Exploring Words

■ Read each sentence. Fill in the circle next to the best meaning for the word in dark print. If you need help, use the Glossary.

1. At first, people thought airships were **marvelous**.
   o a. silly   o b. great   o c. dangerous

2. The Hindenburg was a German **airship**.
   o a. ship that floats in the air
   o b. ship that runs underwater
   o c. car

3. **Hydrogen** made the Hindenburg lighter than air.
   o a. wind   o b. wax   o c. gas

4. The crew wanted to **prevent** a fire.
   o a. avoid   o b. build   o c. watch

5. People did not expect the **blimp** to blow up.
   o a. airship   o b. gas   o c. boat

6. **Static electricity** might have started the fire.
   o a. lightning   o b. magnet   o c. an electric charge

7. Crew members wore suits made of special **fabric**.
   o a. cloth   o b. oil   o c. color

8. Captain Pruss didn't want to **risk** landing in bad weather.
   o a. reward   o b. take the chance of   o c. tell about

9. Some people were left with **injuries**.
   o a. burns   o b. children   o c. pictures

10. Today, airships use **helium**.
    o a. liquid   o b. a safe gas   o c. water

Tidal Wave!

The men in the Alaskan lighthouse looked at each other in surprise. They felt a strange trembling.

"What's that?" asked one.

The other men **shrugged**. It was 2:00 A.M. on April 1, 1946. The men didn't know that the trembling was caused by an earthquake. The earthquake caused a huge **tidal wave**. The tidal wave was rushing through the ocean toward them.

By the time it reached them, it **towered** 115 feet in the air. It crashed over the lighthouse. The lighthouse and the men inside were swept away.

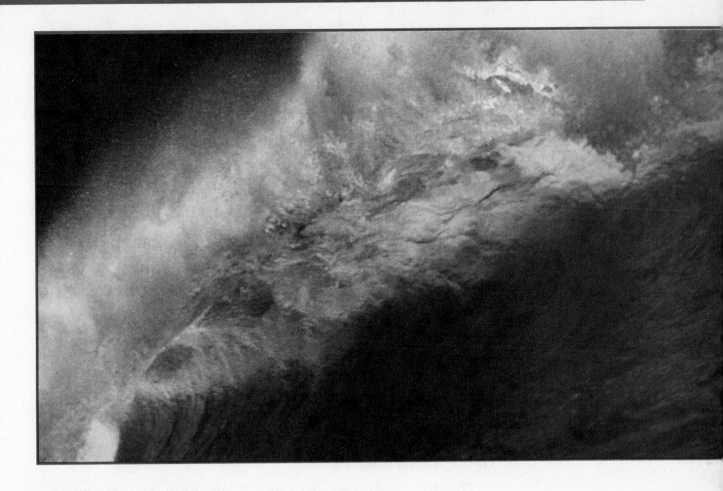

An Earthquake

The tidal wave, or **tsunami**, the Japanese word for *storm wave*, was caused by an earthquake deep in the Pacific Ocean. The earthquake shifted the ocean floor. It sent a huge wave traveling across the water. The wave rippled out in a wide **arc**. It gained speed as it went. Soon it hit Alaska. Then it struck the west coast of Canada and the United States. But the Hawaiian Islands took the worst beating.

A Giant Wave

Captain W.R. Wickland was aboard a navy ship in Hilo Harbor on the island of Hawaii. Around 6:50 A.M., he noticed something strange. The ship dropped a bit. Then it rose. It happened again.

"I looked out and saw what looked like a low, long **swell** at sea coming in awfully fast. I was some 46 feet above water line. That wave was just about eye-level."

Wickland tried to get the ship away from the **dock**. But the whole harbor emptied as the giant wave sucked out all the water. Wickland remembers looking out to see **coral reefs** around the ship.

The harbor filled and emptied four times as Wickland watched. Luckily, the ship's stern was pointed out to sea. That helped the ship ride out the giant wave.

The Lucky Ones

Fusai Tsutsumi was at home in the city of Hilo, Hawaii when the wave hit. She looked up in surprise as her sister burst into the room. "Come see the river! It goes so fast!"

The two girls ran outside. They saw several boys biking as fast as they could. The boys yelled, "Tidal wave! Tidal wave!"

The sisters ran back inside the house to warn their brother. He just laughed. He thought it was an April Fool's Day joke.

The three of them looked out the window. They saw people and debris washing down the river. That was when they realized the danger. This was no April Fool's Day joke! They dashed outside. They ran to a nearby soft drink bottling plant. The concrete building saved them and many of their neighbors.

The Not-So-Lucky Ones

The children of the Laupahoehoe School were not so lucky. Many arrived at school early. They played

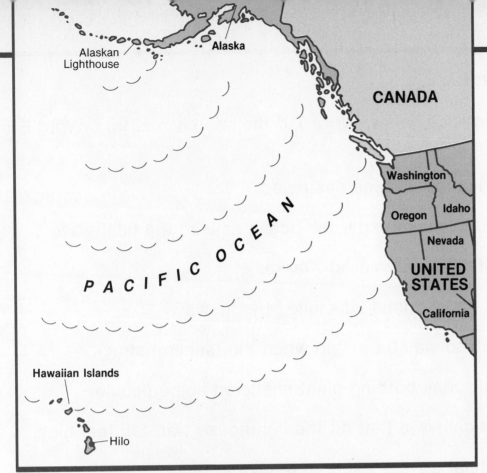

This map shows the path of the tidal wave.

on a field just inside the **sea wall**. Other students were riding down the hill in their school bus. They saw the sea draw back. They couldn't believe their eyes. The ocean floor was bare. All the water had been sucked out to feed the tidal wave. When the bus stopped, students rushed to the sea wall. The strange sight thrilled them.

Suddenly, an ever-rising wall of water appeared. The students screamed in terror. They ran for their lives. Some made it. Others were swallowed by the wave and never seen again.

In all, the tidal wave killed 159 people in the Hawaiian Islands. Property damage was about $26 million. Scientists are now able to give warnings of tidal waves. They study earthquake **tremors** to measure how long after an earthquake a tidal wave will hit. Their warnings will help save many lives.

Do You Remember?

■ Read each sentence below. Write **T** if the sentence is true. Write **F** if the sentence is false.

_____ 1. The lighthouse was destroyed.

_____ 2. An earthquake under the ocean caused the tidal wave.

_____ 3. The tidal wave missed Alaska.

_____ 4. Captain Wickland was killed by the wave.

_____ 5. Wickland was on a ship when the tsunami struck.

_____ 6. A soft drink bottling plant sheltered some people.

_____ 7. The tidal wave that hit the lighthouse was 115 feet high.

_____ 8. The tidal wave sucked all the water out of Hilo Harbor.

Critical Thinking — Finding the Sequence

■ Number the sentences to show the order in which things happened in the story. The first one is done for you.

_____ The children ran for their lives.

_____ The bus stopped at the Laupahoehoe School.

___1___ The ocean floor shifted.

_____ The tidal wave struck Alaska.

_____ The children saw the bare ocean floor.

Exploring Words

■ Use the words in the box to complete the paragraphs. Reread the paragraphs to be sure they make sense.

sea wall	tidal wave	arc	swell	shrugged
tsunami	towered	dock	tremors	coral reefs

When the trembling started, the men in the lighthouse

(1) _____. They didn't know a (2) _____

was coming. The giant wave spread out in an (3) _____

Another word for tidal wave is (4) _____. The wave

(5) _____ 115 feet in the air.

From far away, the tidal wave looked like a low (6) _____

in the water. But in fact it was huge. Ships near the

(7) _____ were in danger. The tidal wave

sucked the water out of the harbor. Because of this,

(8) _____ could be seen on the floor of the ocean.

The wave also swept away some children standing near a

(9) _____

Scientists study earthquake (10) _____ so that they

can warn people of approaching tidal waves.

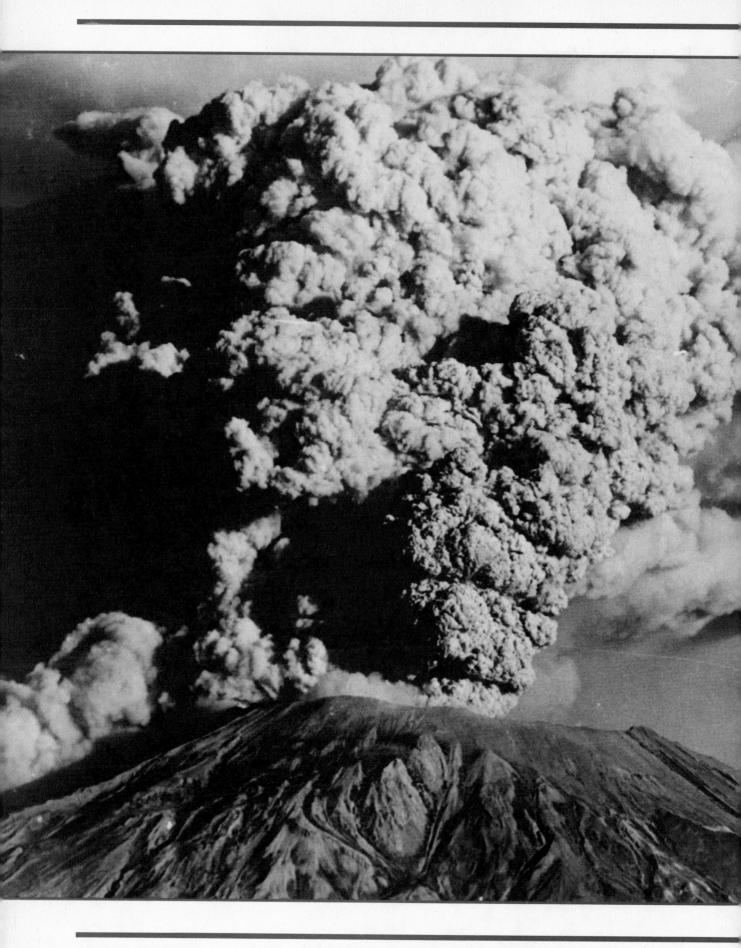

A Mountain Erupts

David Johnston, a **volcano** expert, stared into his **binoculars**. There it was! He could see the lump on the side of the mountain. It was getting bigger. Any moment now it would **erupt**.

"Vancouver, Vancouver, this is it!" He radioed to scientists 50 miles away.

It was exactly 8:31 A.M. on May 18, 1980. Seconds later, Mount St. Helens exploded.

Johnston had wanted to get a good look at Mount St. Helens. So he climbed to a spot five miles away from the mountain. It wasn't far enough. He was never heard from again.

A Waiting Game

The experts knew that Mount St. Helens near Vancouver, Washington, would blow up. The only question was when. A small eruption took place on March 27, 1980. For the next eight weeks, the volcano steamed and rumbled. People everywhere followed the reports day by day.

The people who lived in the area were warned of the danger. They were told to leave while they still could. Many people, however, did not want to leave. George Pickett, a **logger**, lived with his family on nearby Toutle River. He and 200 other loggers were supposed to cut trees near the mountain on Monday, May 19.

Luckily, Pickett was at home Sunday morning. He heard a noise. At first, he thought someone was rolling barrels down the road. "There was a roar, like a jet plane approaching, and a lot of snapping and popping. Those were the trees. We got out fast."

Two campers on the Toutle River were not so lucky. They woke up to a rumbling sound. They ran to their car. But the river flooded the road and kept them from leaving. They climbed on top of the car just as a mud slide crashed toward them. The mud pushed the car into the river. The pair fell into the hot, muddy water. Logs almost crushed them. They were carried about a mile down the river. Finally, a family of campers saved them.

I Want to Live

The power of a volcano is hard to imagine. This one had 500 times the force of a bomb. The blast blew 1,200 feet off the top of the mountain. It shot ash twelve miles into the sky. The volcano also

caused giant mud slides. These mud slides destroyed everything in their path.

David Crockett, a **photographer** for a TV station, happened to be in the wrong place at the wrong time. He was on a dirt road at the bottom of Mount St. Helens. All of a sudden, he heard the blast. He looked up. He saw a huge wall of hot mud. It was rushing straight toward him.

Luckily, the river of mud split in two. It shot past him on both sides of the road. Ash filled the air and made it hard for him to breathe. All he could do was to keep walking down the road. He recorded what was happening.

"I am walking toward the only light I can see. I can hear the mountain rumble. At this very moment I have to say I believe I am dead. The ash burns my eyes! It's very, very hard to breathe and very dark. If I could only breathe air. I will try the radio. Mayday! Mayday! Ash is coming down on me heavily. I want to live!"

Crockett made it out alive. A **helicopter** saved him. But by that time, he had spent ten long hours wondering if he would die.

A Wasteland

The volcano killed 60 people. The mud slides wiped out 123 homes. They also destroyed bridges, roads, and wildlife. Over 150 square miles of trees

were flattened. Lumber companies lost about $500 million. In nearby lakes and streams, fish died by the millions. The eruption turned the whole area into a **wasteland**. President Jimmy Carter viewed the damage. He said, "The moon looks like a golf course compared to what's up there."

The volcanic ash caused other problems. People 100 miles away could barely breathe. They had to wear **masks** over their mouths. Some towns had several inches of ash on the streets. One writer wrote, "Spokane looked like an ashtray."

But it could have been much worse. Some volcanos have caused much more damage. Luckily, not many people lived near Mount St. Helens. And this volcano was only **average** in size. Still, Mount St. Helens was large enough to remind us of how **powerful** nature is.

Do You Remember?

■ Read each sentence below. Write **T** if the sentence is true. Write **F** if the sentence is false.

_____ 1. No one expected Mt. St. Helens to blow up.

_____ 2. George Pickett and his family escaped from the volcano.

_____ 3. Ash was shot twelve miles into the sky.

_____ 4. David Crockett died in a boiling sea of mud.

_____ 5. Ash filled the air and made it hard to breathe.

_____ 6. The volcano caused huge mud slides.

_____ 7. This was the first time damage had been caused by a volcano.

_____ 8. People 100 miles away could feel the effects of the volcano.

Express Yourself

■ Pretend you are David Crockett. You have just been rescued after spending ten hours trapped near the volcano. Describe to your family what happened and how you feel.

_____

_____

_____

_____

_____

_____

Exploring Words

■ Use the clues to complete the puzzle. Choose from the words in the box.

volcano	binoculars	erupt	logger
photographer	helicopter	wasteland	mask
average	powerful		

Across

2. a person who takes pictures
6. glasses used to see things far away
7. an exploding mountain
9. a cover used to protect the face
10. a person who cuts down trees

Down

1. to explode
3. aircraft without wings
4. strong
5. an empty or destroyed place
8. medium size

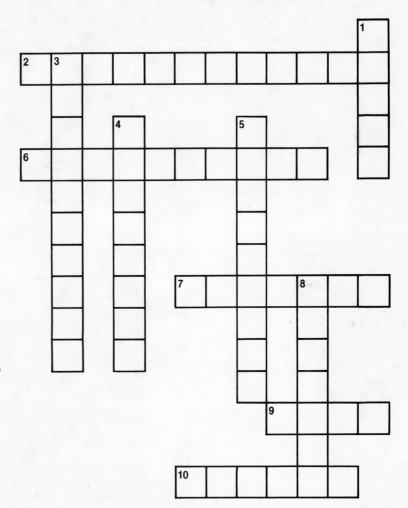

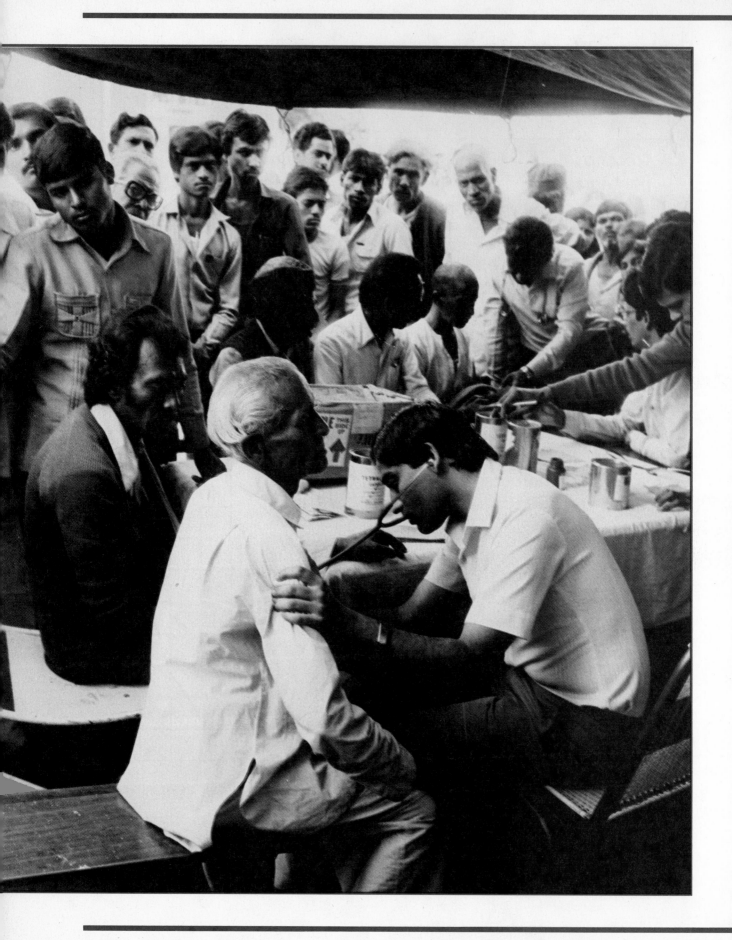

A Cloud of Death

The cloud hit Bhopal, India, at one o'clock in the morning. At that hour, most people were asleep. The night air was cool. The streets were empty. A calmness hung over the city of 900,000 people. Suddenly, the calmness was **shattered**.

Some people awoke with watering eyes. Others felt sharp pains in their chests. Still others felt a stinging in their noses. Within minutes, everyone was suffering the same **agony**. A huge white cloud of poison gas came down upon the city. Before the night was over, it would bring pain and death to thousands of people.

Breathing Fire

The poison gas which formed the cloud was **methyl isocyanate**. It was one **chemical** used in a nearby Union Carbide **plant**. Plant workers kept the chemical in a sealed 45-ton tank. But on December 3, 1984, the tank sprang a leak. The chemical escaped. It formed a **deadly** cloud of gas that covered Bhopal. The gas mixed with **moisture** in people's bodies. It burned their eyes and their lungs.

"It was like breathing fire," said one man.

"It was like a big gas chamber," said another.

A City in Pain

People did not know what had happened. Many thought a war had broken out. As many as 200,000 people poured into the streets. They ran for their lives. The streets were soon packed. Hundreds of people died as they tried to run away. Those still standing were too blind to see where they were going.

Some people did make it to the train station. But the trains could not move. No one could run them.

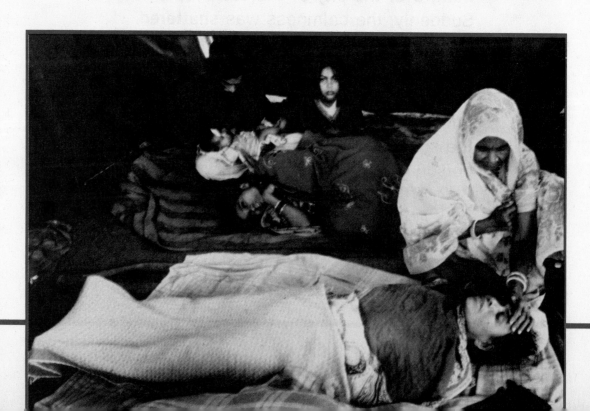

Railroad workers lay on the ground in pain. They too had breathed in the poison gas.

By the next morning, the deadly cloud had broken up and vanished. But the damage was done. About 2,500 people lay dead. Over 100,000 were badly injured. Some suffered kidney infections. Others had brain damage. Thousands lost their eyesight. And many were left with terrible lung problems.

At nearby hospitals, doctors did what they could. But there wasn't much they could do. There is no known cure for methyl isocyanate poisoning.

Searching for Answers

Back at Union Carbide, officials tried to find out what had gone wrong. Why had the giant chemical tank sprung a leak? And why hadn't workers been able to stop it? They found that the leak was caused by a broken **valve**. Safety measures to deal with a leak had not worked.

Some workers tried to control the leak after it began. But they were not able to seal the tank. Tons of the deadly chemical **billowed** into the air. Nearly an hour passed before the tank was finally sealed.

The Bhopal disaster alarmed people around the world. Many questions were raised. What was to keep such an accident from happening at other chemical plants? How safe were the people who lived near these plants? How could safety systems be improved?

These questions were not easily answered. Union Carbide agreed to pay $470 million to the people of Bhopal. But money could not repair the damage. Bhopal serves as a sad reminder of the dangers of **technology**.

The Union Carbide plant that is in Bhopal, India.

63

Do You Remember?

■ In the blank, write the letter of the best ending for each sentence.

_____ 1. When the deadly gas hit Bhopal, most people were
   a. at work.   b. on vacation.   c. sleeping.

_____ 2. The poison gas came from a nearby
   a. chemical plant.   b. school.   c. hospital.

_____ 3. People tried to
   a. hide.   b. run away.   c. talk about it.

_____ 4. The leak in the tank was finally sealed in
   a. twelve hours.   b. an hour.   c. a day.

_____ 5. By the next morning, the deadly cloud was
   a. bigger.   b. moving south.   c. gone.

Critical Thinking — Cause and Effect

■ Complete the following sentences.

1. People awoke in the middle of the night because_____

_____

2. The chemical escaped because _____

_____

3. The trains could not move because _____

_____

4. Doctors could not do much to help because _____

_____

_____

Exploring Words

■ Use the words in the box to complete the paragraph. Reread the paragraph to be sure it makes sense.

agony	plant	moisture	chemical	technology
valve	deadly	billowed	shattered	methyl isocyanate

Most people in Bhopal were sleeping when a cloud formed. The cloud **(1)** _____ the calmness of the night. The cloud was formed by a **(2)** _____ called **(3)** _____ _____. It **(4)** _____ out of a Union Carbide **(5)** _____. The **(6)** _____ gas leaked out when a **(7)** _____ broke. The poison gas caused the people of Bhopal much **(8)** _____. The gas mixed with **(9)** _____ in their bodies. People everywhere were reminded of the dangers of **(10)** _____.

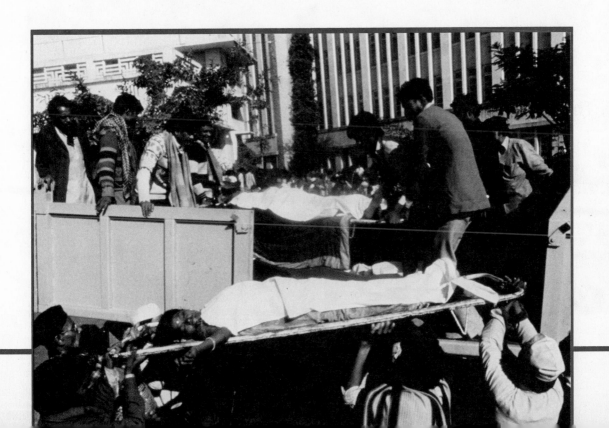

Last Flight of the Challenger

The school children jumped up and down in the field. They were excited and couldn't wait for the big moment to arrive.

"We're at nine minutes and counting," the announcer said.

The children turned their eyes to the Cape Canaveral **launch** pad just four miles away. There sat the space **shuttle** Challenger. In a few minutes, it would blast off.

"T minus four minutes and counting."

The children giggled. These third-graders had never been so excited. Their classmate's mother was on board the shuttle. Her name was Christa McAuliffe. She was a teacher in their hometown of Concord, New Hampshire. She was the first teacher ever to go up into space.

"T minus ten . . . nine . . . eight . . . seven . . . six . . ."

Silence fell over the field.

"We have main-engine start."

The children held their breath.

A Delayed Launch

Christa McAuliffe had been waiting for this day for over a year. It started when she entered a contest. More than 11,000 teachers entered. They all wanted to ride the shuttle. But McAuliffe won. McAuliffe was bright, daring, and full of spirit. She was the perfect person to go up in the Challenger. She would show everyone that space travel was safe and fun.

McAuliffe couldn't fly the shuttle, of course. She was a passenger. The shuttle would be flown by six **astronauts**. Dick Scobee would be the flight **commander**. Scobee had already made one trip in the shuttle. So had three of the other astronauts.

NASA was in charge of the flight. NASA is the National **Aeronautics** and Space Administration. It runs America's space program. NASA planned the launch for January 25, 1986. But bad weather forced a **delay**. Then there was a problem with the shuttle's door. Again the date was pushed back.

January 28 was a very cold day. The shuttle had never been launched in such cold weather. Some scientists were worried. They thought the cold

Back row: El Onizuka, Christa McAuliffe, Greg Jarvis, Judy Resnik.
Front row: Mike Smith, Dick Scobee, Ron McNair.

weather could cause trouble. They feared it might damage the shuttle's O-rings. These rings sealed the rocket boosters. Other scientists disagreed. They thought the shuttle would be fine. NASA decided to go ahead with the launch.

Disaster Strikes

"Four . . . three . . . two . . . one. And liftoff!" the announcer said. "Liftoff of the twenty-fifth space shuttle mission. And it has cleared the tower."

The children watching from the field broke into wild cheers. They danced with joy. They saw the shuttle move up, up, up into the sky.

On board the Challenger, McAuliffe and the others lay in place. The power of the blast-off pushed them deep into their seats. Commander Scobee talked on the radio with the control tower. At first, everything seemed normal. After 52 seconds, a **controller** told Scobee that everything looked fine.

"Challenger, go with **throttle** up," the controller said.

"Roger, go with throttle up," Scobee replied.

Scobee's words were spoken 70 seconds into the flight. Four seconds later, something horrible happened. Red, yellow, and orange flames shot out from the shuttle. The Challenger turned into a ball of fire. Then it exploded into many pieces.

We Will Remember

Back on Earth, no one could believe it. Some of the children in the field began crying. McAuliffe's family stared in **horror**. The controllers in the tower didn't know what to say. All around the world, people sat in shock.

People expressed their **grief** in many ways. Some kept their porch lights burning in memory of the shuttle crew. Others put up signs which read, May They Rest in Peace. President Reagan honored them in a speech. Pope John Paul II said a special prayer. Everywhere people cried and prayed and hugged each other.

Later a commission explored why the shuttle had exploded. Photographs showed dark smoke coming from the right rocket booster seconds after liftoff. It appeared that the O-rings had failed to work.

The Challenger explodes.

Flags at the White House honor the astronauts.

Everyone was upset. NASA did not launch another shuttle for more than two years. It worked to make sure that such a mistake would never happen again.

The Challenger disaster reminded everyone of the risks of space travel. Ronald McNair was one of the astronauts on board the Challenger. Earlier he had said, "You can only become a winner if you are willing to walk over the edge." For their willingness to face the unknown, the crew of the Challenger will always be remembered.

Do You Remember?

■ In the blank, write the letter of the best ending for each sentence.

_____ 1. Christa McAuliffe was a
   a. scientist.   b. teacher.   c. engineer.

_____ 2. Christa McAuliffe wanted to show that space travel was
   a. hard.   b. dangerous.   c. fun.

_____ 3. Dick Scobee was the flight
   a. announcer.   b. commander.   c. controller.

_____ 4. The shuttle had never been launched in such
   a. cold weather.   b. wind.   c. rain.

_____ 5. When the shuttle exploded, people were
   a. shocked.   b. thrilled.   c. calm.

Express Yourself

■ Explain what Ronald McNair meant when he said, "You can only become a winner if you are willing to walk over the edge." Write about whether or not you agree.

_____

_____

_____

_____

_____

_____

_____

Exploring Words

■ Use the clues to complete the puzzle. Choose from the words in the box.

launch
shuttle
astronauts
commander
Aeronautics
delay
controller
throttle
horror
grief

Across
3. The <u>Challenger</u> was a space _____.
6. first "A" in "NASA"
7. to change to a later time
9. great sadness
10. lever to control speed

Down
1. Dick Scobee's job
2. he talked to astronauts by radio
4. to take off
5. people who travel in space
8. great fear

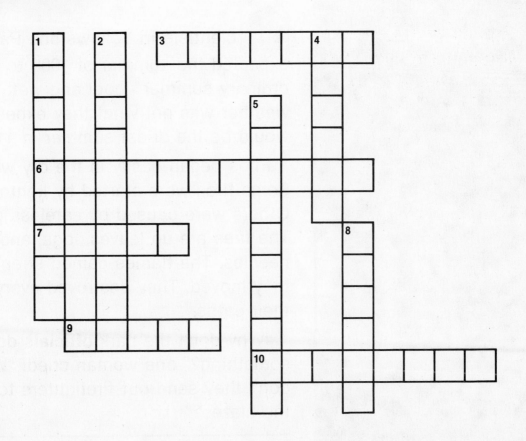

A Park in Flames

Scientists in Yellowstone Park expected the summer of 1988 to be an ordinary summer - cool and wet. But the weather was not what they expected. This would be the driest summer in 112 years.

Fires began easily in the dry weather. Some fires were started by lightning. Others were caused by careless people. The fires ate up leaves, logs, and pine needles. The flames gained strength as they moved. They destroyed everything in their paths.

"Why don't the park **officials** do something?" one woman cried. "Why don't they send out firefighters to stop the blazes?"

Park Policy

For over one hundred years the National Park Service had fought all fires in Yellowstone as soon as they started. But **scientists** began to feel that this was a mistake. They thought that fires were nature's way of cleaning out the forest.

In 1972, park **policy** changed. The Park Service would fight fires started by humans. Fires started **naturally** by lightning would be allowed to burn. Only if natural fires **threatened** lives or property would they be fought. So when the fires in Yellowstone Park began in June, 1988, park officials battled only some of the blazes. But the fires kept growing and growing.

People who lived in nearby towns complained that the fires were burning out of control. They feared the fires would drive away the **tourists**. "We'd see the fire get bigger and bigger, and they wouldn't do a thing about it," said one motel owner.

Out of Control

On July 21, Yellowstone officials declared war on all fires in the park. By then, the fires were huge. The flames threatened buildings and tourist centers.

Nine thousand firefighters poured into Yellowstone. Some came in helicopters. They tried to fight the fire from the air. Others stayed on the ground. They came with **bulldozers** and chain saws. They hurried to clear wide strips of land. The workers hoped these strips would stop the fires.

Day after day, the firefighters battled the flames. But they could not put them out. The weather was just too dry and windy.

The Battle Continues

On September 9, the fires were still burning. Firefighters fought to save the historic park buildings. They sprayed the famous Old Faithful Inn with water and chemicals. The 200-foot wall of flames roared closer. The firefighters ran to safety. When the smoke cleared, they were glad to see that the hotel still stood. The large parking lot around it had protected it.

By mid-September, Yellowstone Park was completely closed to visitors. Many people **criticized** the Park Service. They thought officials had waited too long to begin fighting the fires.

Others blamed the high winds and drought. Of the thirteen big fires in Yellowstone, eight had been fought from the start. All eight were still burning. "Even with every **weapon**, men cannot always put out a wildfire," one official said.

As the fall weather set in, the fires did slow down. But they didn't die until the November snow came. It

was nature itself that finally put out the blazes. By then, one-fifth of the park had been blackened.

Some people thought the fires were a terrible disaster. They felt that park officials should have acted more quickly. But scientists disagreed.

"These fires are natural **events**," said scientist James Schmitt. Scientists thought that in the long run the fires might be good for the park. The flames burned the biggest, driest trees. That left room for new trees to grow.

Whether good or bad, the results of the summer of 1988 will be with us for many years.

Do You Remember?

■ Read each sentence below. Write **T** if the sentence is true. Write **F** if the sentence is false.

1. _____ The summer of 1988 was very wet in Yellowstone.

2. _____ Some of the fires were started by lightning.

3. _____ Gusts of wind made the fires easier to control.

4. _____ The Park Service policy was to only fight fires started by humans.

5. _____ Firefighters tried to stop the fires by clearing strips of land.

6. _____ The famous Old Faithful Inn was completely destroyed.

7. _____ Nine thousand firefighters could not put out the fires.

8. _____ The fires were finally put out by snow in November.

Critical Thinking—Finding the Sequence

■ Number the sentences to show the order in which things happened in the story. The first one is done for you.

_____ Many firefighters came in to fight the fires.

_____ Fires were started by lightning and careless people.

_____ The fires died out when the winter snows came.

_____ Yellowstone officials declared war on the fires.

__1__ Scientists expected 1988 to be cool and wet.

Exploring Words

■ Write the correct word in each sentence.

officials	threatened	policy	tourist	criticized
bulldozers	scientists	weapon	events	naturally

1. Machines that move dirt are called _____.

2. _____ are things that happen.

3. People who study science are _____.

4. The rules or _____ about fighting fires changed in 1972.

5. People who are in charge of something are called

   _____.

6. A _____ travels to places for fun.

7. To be put in danger is to be _____.

8. A _____ is something to fight with.

9. If something happens _____, it is caused by nature.

10. People _____ or found fault with the Park Service.

Hurricane Warning!

Señor Garcia stood at the window. He saw waves tossing and **thrashing**.

"We must go," he whispered to his wife. "The **hurricane** is coming!"

"No, I will never leave my home," she said.

So the two of them stayed in the little village of La Carbonera, Mexico. The weather grew wilder. The wind reached 120 miles per hour. Señor Garcia had never seen a storm so full of **fury**.

Suddenly, the hurricane tore into the Garcias' house. It ripped off the roof and knocked down walls. Somehow, Señor Garcia escaped injury. But his wife lost her life in the storm.

The Power of Gilbert

Hurricane Gilbert was the worst storm to come out of the Atlantic Ocean in 80 years. It began off the coast of Africa in September, 1988. At first, it was only a small **cluster** of thunderclouds. But it gathered strength as it moved over open water. It picked up heat and moisture. When it reached the Caribbean Islands, it was a **monster**.

By then the storm stretched over 450 miles. It carried heavy rain and strong winds. At the eye of the storm, the wind reached hurricane level. It measured an amazing 175 miles per hour.

This wind was deadly. It smashed buildings. It ripped up telephone poles and street lights. It sent

25-foot waves crashing onto beaches. It even carried a big ship for five miles and dumped it onto the sand.

Jamaica's Nightmare

The island of Jamaica caught the worst of the storm. There the wind tore the roofs off 80 **percent** of all homes. It left half a million people homeless. It also destroyed crops. Banana trees, coconut trees, and sugar cane plants were ruined.

As Gilbert approached Jamaica on September 12, tourists rushed to get off the island. Many made it. But hundreds did not. Those who were stuck on the island gathered in big hotels. But even there they were not safe. The storm shattered hotel windows. It broke down walls. It sent furniture flying.

"It was like being hit by an atom bomb," one tourist later said.

"Sixty-foot trees were just **plucked** out of the earth," another said.

One man summed it up. "There was no power, no water, no phones, nothing. The place was wrecked."

After leaving Jamaica, Gilbert raced through the Cayman Islands. Then it rushed on to Mexico. There the howling wind and rain did new damage. The storm leveled thousands more homes. It flipped cars and ruined roads. And it flooded mile after mile of land.

Death of a Hurricane

On September 17, Gilbert finally lost its great strength. The wind died down. The rain grew lighter. But **evidence** of the storm remained. It had caused billions of dollars in damages. Over 800,000 people had no homes. The death count reached 300.

But things could have been worse. In the past, a hurricane like Gilbert would have killed thousands of people. It would have hit without warning. There would have been no way to **predict** its path.

This time, at least, everyone knew Gilbert was coming. Weather experts used new tools to study Gilbert's path. These experts sent out plenty of warnings. The warnings gave many people time to **flee**. Others could at least try to protect themselves and their property from the wind. Luckily, most people lived through Hurricane Gilbert. They were able to dry out and start again after the fury of Gilbert had passed.

Do You Remember?

■ In the blank, write the letter of the best ending for each sentence.

_____ 1. Hurricane Gilbert began off the coast of
a. Canada.   b. China.   c. Africa.

_____ 2. The hurricane did the most damage in
a. England.   b. Jamaica.   c. New Mexico.

_____ 3. Hurricane Gilbert destroyed Jamaica's crop of
a. bananas.   b. potatoes.   c. rice.

_____ 4. The hurricane caused
a. snowdrifts.   b. flooding.   c. fires.

_____ 5. Weather experts were able to give people
a. raincoats.   b. free food.   c. warning.

Express Yourself

■ Pretend that you are a tourist in Jamaica. You were trapped on the island by Hurricane Gilbert. Write a letter to a friend telling what happened and how you felt.

Dear _____,

_____

_____

_____

_____

_____

_____

_____

_____

Exploring Words

■ Find the best meaning for the word in dark print. Fill in the circle next to it.

1. The word **thrashing** means
   ○ a. moving wildly.   ○ b. cooking.   ○ c. singing.

2. The word **hurricane** means
   ○ a. hard candy.   ○ b. high speed.   ○ c. a bad windstorm.

3. The word **fury** means
   ○ a. wild and dangerous force.
   ○ b. ready to eat.
   ○ c. striped.

4. The word **cluster** means
   ○ a. dirty.   ○ b. a group of something.   ○ c. a ring.

5. The word **monster** means
   ○ a. lost.   ○ b. huge.   ○ c. sandstorm.

6. The word **percent** means
   ○ a. out of each hundred.   ○ b. buy.   ○ c. gift.

7. The word **plucked** means
   ○ a. painted.   ○ b. tired.   ○ c. pulled out.

8. The word **evidence** means
   ○ a. proof.   ○ b. whirlwinds.   ○ c. trash.

9. The word **predict** means
   ○ a. spend time in jail.
   ○ b. tell what will happen.
   ○ c. win a bet.

10. The word **flee** means
    ○ a. fly.   ○ b. run away.   ○ c. doesn't cost money.

Glossary

acres, page 5

An acre is equal to 43,560 square feet. This is a little smaller than the size of a football field.

aeronautics, page 68

Aeronautics is the science of building and flying a spacecraft.

agony, page 61

Agony is great pain.

airship, page 38

An airship is a type of balloon that can be steered.

arc, page 47

An arc is part of a circle.

astronauts, page 68

Astronauts are people who travel in space.

average, page 57

Average means of a medium size.

billow, page 63

Billow means to flow out in large amounts.

binoculars, page 53

Binoculars are like two telescopes that have been joined together. They are used to look at things far away.

blimp, page 40

A blimp is a type of balloon that can be steered.

blizzard, page 10

A blizzard is a long, heavy snowstorm.

bow, page 35

The bow is the front part of a ship.

bulldozer, page 76

A bulldozer is a tractor with wide steel blades. Bulldozers push rocks and earth.

chemical, page 62

A chemical is made when two or more kinds of matter are mixed.

clung, page 18

If you clung to something, you held on tightly.

cluster, page 81

Cluster means a group of something.

commander, page 68

A commander is the person in charge.

compartments, page 32

Compartments are separate rooms.

controller, page 70

A controller is the person who directs something.

coral reefs, page 48

Coral reefs are thin lines of stony material. They are found near the surface of the water.

courthouse, page 3

A courthouse is a building where courts of law and county offices are.

crisis, page 27

A crisis is a time of difficulty.

criticize, page 76

It you criticize something, you find fault with it.

current, page 19

A current is a moving body of water.

dam, page 17

A dam is a wall built to hold back water.

deadly, page 62

When something is deadly, it can cause death.

death, page 19

Death is the ending of life.

debris, page 19

Debris is the trash left when something has been destroyed.

delay, page 68

A delay puts off something for a time.

disaster

A disaster is something that happens suddenly and causes suffering and loss.

dock, page 48

A dock is a raised surface built out from the shore.

drought, page 4

A drought is a long period of dry weather with little or no rain.

dynamite, page 27

Dynamite is used to blow things up.

earthquake, page 24

An earthquake is a movement of the earth's crust.

eerie, page 12

Something eerie is strange and frightening.

embers, page 4

Embers are pieces of wood or coal still glowing from a fire.

enterprise, page 17

An enterprise is a business.

erupt, page 53

To erupt means to explode violently.

events, page 77

Events are things that happen.

evidence, page 82

Evidence is proof of something.

fabric, page 42

Fabric is cloth or material.

fiercely, page 4

Fiercely means forcefully and wildly.

flakes, page 10

Flakes are small, thin bits of snow.

fled, page 4

If someone fled from a place, that person ran away.

flee, page 83

Flee means to run away.

flung, page 12

When something is flung, it is thrown hard.

forbid, page 27

To forbid is to order people not to do something.

freak, page 10.

A freak happening is something which is unusual.

fury, page 80

Fury means a wild and dangerous force.

grief, page 70

Grief is a great sadness. When someone dies, you feel grief.

gust, page 9

A gust is a sudden, strong blast of wind.

helicopter, page 56

A helicopter is an aircraft without wings. It is kept in the air by propellers.

helium, page 43

Helium is a light gas that will not burn.

horror, page 70

Horror is great fear or shock.

hurricane, page 80

A hurricane is a bad storm that starts in the ocean. It has winds above 75 miles per hour, heavy rains, thunder, and lightning.

hydrant, page 25

A hydrant is a pipe that brings water. Firefighters attach their hoses to hydrants when they fight fires.

hydrogen, page 41

Hydrogen is a light gas that burns easily.

icebergs, page 31

Icebergs are large chunks of ice that float in the ocean.

icicles, page 13

When dripping water freezes, it forms spikes of ice called icicles.

injuries, page 43

Injuries are damages or losses suffered. Burns were some of the injuries suffered by the people on the Hindenburg.

lack, page 4

Lack means not to have enough of something.

lantern, page 2

A lantern is a lamp with glass sides which can be carried.

launch, page 67

A launch is the act of sending a space shuttle into the air.

lifeboats, page 32

Lifeboats are small boats. They are used for saving lives at sea.

logger, page 54

A logger is a person who cuts down trees, saws them into logs, and moves them out of the forest.

lookout, page 31

A lookout is a person who watches for danger.

looting, page 27
Looting is stealing.

marvelous, page 38
Marvelous means wonderful.

mask, page 57
A mask is a cover for the face used for protection.

methyl isocyanate, page 62
Methyl isocyanate is a poison used to kill insects.

moisture, page 62
Moisture is wetness.

monster, page 81
A monster is something unusually large.

naturally, page 75
If something happens naturally, it is caused by nature.

nightmare, page 17
A nightmare is a frightening dream.

officials, page 74
Officials are people who are in charge of something.

percent, page 82
Percent means parts in each hundred. Eighty percent means eighty of each hundred.

photographer, page 55
A photographer is a person whose job is taking pictures with a camera.

plant, page 62
A plant is a factory.

plucked, page 82
Plucked means pulled out quickly.

policy, page 75
A policy is a set of rules.

powerful, page 57
Powerful means having great force.

predict, page 83
Predict means to tell about something before it happens.

prevent, page 41
If you try to prevent something, you try to keep it from happening.

raging, page 18
When something is raging, it is moving wildly with a great force.

refugees, page 26
Refugees are people who leave their homes because their lives are in danger.

retire, page 31
When people retire, they stop working. Many people retire when they are 65.

risk, page 40
Risk means to take a chance.

rubble, page 24
Broken stones or bricks are rubble.

ruins, page 5
Ruins means an area that has been so badly damaged that it is destroyed.

scientist, page 75

A scientist is a person who studies nature and other areas of science.

sea wall, page 49

A sea wall is a strong wall built to keep sea waves from wearing away the shore.

shatter, page 61

When something shatters, it breaks.

shingle, page 5

A shingle is a thin piece of wood used to cover a roof or wall.

shock, page 24

When you are shocked, you are so surprised that you cannot do or say anything.

shortage, page 34

When there is a shortage, there is not enough of something.

shrug, page 46

If you shrug your shoulders, you raise your shoulders to show that you don't understand something.

shuttle, page 67

A shuttle travels back and forth over a certain route.

sleet, page 13

Sleet is frozen rain.

snowdrifts, page 10

Snowdrifts are piles of snow formed by the wind.

static electricity, page 42

Static electricity is an electric charge in the air. The charge is made by two things rubbing together. If you walk across a carpet and get a shock when you touch metal, it is caused by static electricity.

stern, page 35

The stern is the back part of a ship.

swell, page 48

A swell is a long ocean wave that moves without breaking.

swirling, page 10

When something is swirling, it is moving with a twisting motion.

technology, page 63

Technology is the use of science to make things and to solve problems.

terrified, page 19

To be terrified is to be very frightened.

thrash, page 80

To thrash is to move wildly.

threaten, page 75

To threaten is to put in danger.

throttle, page 70

A throttle is a valve that controls the flow of fuel to an engine.

tidal wave, page 46

A tidal wave is a huge ocean wave that is caused by an underwater earthquake.

ton, page 18

A ton equals 2,000 pounds.

tourists, page 75

Tourists are people who travel for fun.

tower, page 46

If something towers, it rises up high.

tremor, page 49

A tremor is a shaking movement.

tsunami, page 47

A tsunami is a huge ocean wave caused by an underwater earthquake. A tsunami is the same as a tidal wave.

unsinkable, page 32

A ship is unsinkable if it cannot be made to go underwater.

valve, page 63

A valve controls the flow of something through a pipe.

violently, page 24

Violently means caused by great force.

volcano, page 53

A volcano is a cone-shaped mountain. It is made from lava that has been forced out of the earth. Mount St. Helens is a live volcano.

wasteland, page 57

A wasteland is an empty place where little will grow.

watertight, page 32

Water cannot get in or out of something that is watertight.

weapon, page 76

A weapon is something to fight with.

Chart Your Progress

Stories	Do You Remember?	Exploring Words	Critical Thinking	Express Yourself	Score
Fire! Fire! Fire!				////////	/18
A City Under Snow			////////		/23
Washed Away!				////////	/23
A City in Ruins			////////		/23
Nightmare at Sea				////////	/20
Flames in the Sky!			////////		/20
Tidal Wave!				////////	/23
A Mountain Erupts			////////		/23
A Cloud of Death				////////	/19
Last Flight of the Challenger			////////		/20
A Park in Flames				////////	/23
Hurricane Warning!			////////		/20

Finding Your Score
1. Count the number of correct answers you have for each activity.
2. Write these numbers in the boxes in the chart.
3. Ask your teacher to give you a score (maximum score 5) for **Express Yourself.**
4. Add up the numbers to get a final score.

Answer Key

Fire! Fire! Fire!
Pages 2-7

Do You Remember? 1-b, 2-a, 3-b, 4-a, 5-a

Critical Thinking — Drawing Conclusions:
Answers may vary.
Here are some examples.
1. he wanted to warn them about the fire.
2. a lookout thought the fire was in a different place.
3. they were trying to get away from the fire.

Exploring Words: 1. drought,
2. lack, 3. fiercely, 4. lantern,
5. courthouse, 6. fled, 7. embers,
8. shingles, 9. ruins, 10. acres

A City Under Snow
Pages 8-15

Do You Remember? 1-T, 2-T,
3-F, 4-F, 5-T, 6-F, 7-F, 8-T

Express Yourself: Answers will vary.

Exploring Words: 1-c, 2-b, 3-a,
4-a, 5-b, 6-a, 7-a, 8-c, 9-a, 10-b

Washed Away!
Pages 16-21

Do You Remember? 1-c, 2-a, 3-b, 4-c, 5-b

Critical Thinking — Fact or Opinion?
1-0, 2-F, 3-F, 4-0, 5-F, 6-0, 7-0, 8-F

Exploring Words: Across: 4. current,
5. raging, 6. death, 9. nightmare,
10. debris
Down: 1. clung, 2. terrified,
3. enterprise, 7. ton, 8. dam

A City in Ruins
Pages 22-29

Do You Remember? 1-F, 2-F, 3-T,
4-T, 5-F, 6-T, 7-T, 8-T

Express Yourself: Answers will vary.

Exploring Words: 1. earthquake,
2. violently, 3. shocked, 4. crisis,
5. hydrant, 6. refugees, 7. looting,
8. Forbid, 9. dynamite, 10. rubble

Nightmare at Sea
Pages 30-37

Do You Remember? 1-T, 2-F, 3-T,
4-F, 5-F, 6-F, 7-T, 8-F

Critical Thinking — Main Ideas: 1, 5

Exploring Words: 1. icebergs,
2. shortage, 3. watertight,
4. lookout, 5. bow, 6. lifeboats,
7. unsinkable, 8. Compartments,
9. stern, 10. retire

Flames in the Sky!
Pages 38-45

Do You Remember? 1-a, 2-c,
3-c, 4-a, 5-a

Express Yourself: Answers will vary.

Exploring Words: 1-b, 2-a, 3-c,
4-a, 5-a, 6-c, 7-a, 8-b, 9-a, 10-b

Tidal Wave!
Pages 46-51

Do You Remember? 1-T, 2-T, 3-F,
4-F, 5-T, 6-T, 7-T, 8-T

**Critical Thinking — Finding the
Sequence:** 5, 4, 1, 2, 3

Exploring Words: 1. shrugged,
2. tidal wave/tsunami, 3. arc,
4. tsunami, 5. towered, 6. swell,
7. dock, 8. coral reefs, 9. sea wall,
10. tremors

A Mountain Erupts
Pages 52-59

Do You Remember? 1-F, 2-T, 3-T, 4-F, 5-T, 6-T, 7-F, 8-T

Express Yourself: Answers will vary.

Exploring Words: Across:
2. photographer, 6. binoculars,
7. volcano, 9. mask, 10. logger
Down: 1. erupt, 3. helicopter,
4. powerful, 5. wasteland,
8. average

A Cloud of Death
Pages 60-65

Do You Remember? 1-c, 2-a, 3-b, 4-b, 5-c

Critical Thinking — Cause and Effect:
Answers may vary. Here are some
examples.
1. they were being poisoned by the gas.
2. there was a leak in the tank caused by a broken valve.
3. no one could run them.
4. there is no known cure for this kind of poisoning.

Exploring Words: 1. shattered,
2. chemical, 3. methyl isocyanate,
4. billowed, 5. plant, 6. deadly,
7. valve, 8. agony, 9. moisture,
10. technology

Last Flight of the Challenger
Pages 66-73

Do You Remember? 1-b, 2-c, 3-b, 4-a, 5-a

Express Yourself: Answers will vary.

Exploring Words: Across: 3. shuttle,
6. Aeronautics, 7. delay, 9. grief,
10. throttle
Down: 1. commander, 2. controller,
4. launch, 5. astronauts, 8. horror

A Park in Flames
Pages 74-79

Do You Remember? 1-F, 2-T, 3-F, 4-T, 5-T, 6-F, 7-T, 8-T

**Critical Thinking — Finding the
Sequence:** 4, 2, 5, 3, 1

Exploring Words: 1. bulldozers,
2. Events, 3. scientists, 4. policy,
5. officials, 6. tourist, 7. threatened,
8. weapon, 9. naturally,
10. criticized

Hurricane Warning!
Pages 80-85

Do You Remember? 1-c, 2-b, 3-a, 4-b, 5-c

Express Yourself: Answers will vary.

Exploring Words: 1-a, 2-c, 3-a,
4-b, 5-b, 6-a, 7-c, 8-a, 9-b, 10-b